The Scales
of
Astraea

The Scales of Astraea

Poems
of
Earth, Its Creatures
&
the Old Gods

Djana Bayley

Bywater Press
Bellingham, Washington

Published by Bywater Press, Bellingham, Washington.
www.bywaterpress.com

Printed by CreateSpace.

First edition, first printing.
ISBN: 1974472248
ISBN-13: 978-1974472246

To the memory of
Thais Bayley Bock, 1918–2010
&

Esther Ruth Carson, 1934–2016

Good friends,
passionate advocates of our earth
and all its creatures of land, water and sky.

You are sorely missed.

Contents

Preface

The overarching theme of this book, expressed in each poem, is my love of this earth and the insects, birds, animals, plants and trees that exist on the planet with us. A parallel motif in many of the poems is my perception of the damage inflicted on earth and its creatures by the human race in our haste, ignorance and hubris, with a concomitant awareness of the cruelties – small and large, casual and technological – we are inflicting on the other species living here and to the very earth itself. The harm 'mankind' has imposed on our beautiful planet is immeasurable, the scale nearly incomprehensible – the consequences of our actions with regard to the earth's intricate chain of life are only beginning to manifest.

From the time I was quite young, the myths of the Greek gods fascinated me, and all through my life their interwoven stories have continued to resonate, providing defined points of reference for occurrences in my own life. In certain strange ways – dare I say it? – The Old Gods have even influenced the manner in which I've lived and the roads I've taken through the years.

I am haunted as much today as when a child by those gods and scenes from their lives. To assist in the evocation of my themes, both as particularized symbols and for the potent images still accruing to them, certain of these Immortal Ones – sometimes in their Roman personae – make occasional appearances in the following pages.

I beg their gracious forgiveness for my temerity.

The pastel pencil illustrations were 'drawn by D' over the last two years specifically for this volume.

Djana Bayley, Lynnwood, July 2017

Astraea

In Greek legend, Astraea was considered the daughter of the Titans Astraeus, god of dusk, and Eos, goddess of dawn. When the gods departed earth at the end of the Golden Age, the Star Maiden continued to live among humankind through the Silver Age, a virgin goddess dedicated to upholding natural law, protecting the innocence of all living creatures and the purity of life-sustaining water and soil. In the Age of Bronze, man's increasing cruelty, greed and impiety at last drove her to abandon her earthly realm. On her return to heaven, the gods placed her among the stars as the constellation now known as Virgo; nearby are set her scales: Zygos in Greek, Libra in the Latin.

Depictions of Astraea portray her with a stern but majestic countenance, her head crowned with ears of grain; for its measure she carries in one hand a balance or scale, while in the other she holds a sword.

Note

Greek myth also related that Great Zeus and Themis, a Titaness who established the laws of religion, sacrifice and divination, were parents of Dike, a goddess closely associated – and often confused – with Astraea. Dike was the personification of just judgment regarding human laws, while Astraea always remained the guardian of earth's natural law. The Romans later made Dike their primary goddess of Justice – Justitia – giving her the function of upholding fair judgment among mortals and the keeping of social and political order by strict observance of rights established by custom and law. She was portrayed carrying a sword and scales – her blindfold did not become an attribute until the end of the 15th century.

See Hesiod's *Theogony*, Ovid's *Metamorphoses*, or Virgil's poetry for further details concerning these two goddesses.

Seasons & Birds

Crocuses

On a chill late winter day, gray clouds sagging
with imminent rain, white, lavender, yellow,
blue crocuses lift their in-curved, petal thin
chalices above soaked earth, forming shining

pools of incandescence in grass and bare dirt,
and unfurling rainbow borders glowing
strangely luminous against dark wet trunks and
low sweeping cedar, juniper, fir branches.

Bending close to peer within the upright cups,
translucent as hollow-sculpted alabaster,
I see certain of the purple and blue kind
show inside the silk petals fine striped lines, while

at the core of each, pollen-coated velvet
anthers of powdered orange fire raise
trident-tipped lances straight from the pierced heart
of their unearthly, moon-pearl fluorescence.

Early Swallows

First I hear the twittering and run
outside, shading eyes against pale March
pellucidity, scanning space that has

seemed so empty – starlings, crows, jays, even
finches, chickadees hardly weigh in
like scale – but the sky remains empty and

I begin to doubt my ears (at nearly
two weeks late I fret about hurricanes,
poison sprayings), then again come those fine

electric cries, and this time I find
them – tiny dark scythe-wing specks scribing swift
circles and figure eights high in the cool

blue atmosphere – and day by day the skies
come alive with arrowing, darting swallows
interweaving aerial knots of joyous

arrival down, up, around familiar parks,
roofs, chimneys, trees – the gallant survivors
of that annual storm-tossed, perilous

odyssey from the fabled, farthest Argentine.

The Small Ones

This late in spring – where can these small ones, pretty ones,
flee and chance nesting again? They watch with dark

unwinking eyes as their familiar landscape clawed
and mangled by roaring, reek-spewing metal monsters

smashing, crashing, crawling over their feeding,
hiding, mating coverts. Trembling, they cling on high

wires as their nests, so laboriously built,
their nestlings, so wearily raised, disappear in

a haze of diesel fumes. They cannot understand.
At sunset, huddled too close on unfamiliar perches

in the scant, drooping shrubs left at field's rim, they wait
restless, uneasy. When dawn begins its wan eastern

seep, shapes gradually emerge of a world stripped,
ravaged, changed utterly. The birds do not voice a note or

forage – instead they shift leg to leg, peck a neighbor –
and look with black eyes reflecting pin-point suns at raw

scraped earth, jagged pyramids of crushed blackberry vines,
splintered alder and maple trunks, branches, saplings.

At last, one by one, they unfold feathers – soft-hued green,
gray, russet, tan and brown, bold black, white, flame, gold – and

with slow wingbeats, and some loops back, fly off to seek
other refuges. But their kin have fled before them –

the shrinking interstices of wood edge and pasture
hedge occupied. Few of these pretty ones will survive.

Midsummer Nightmare

The causeless fear that can shake
heart and rock bones flowered inside my blood

one warm jasmine-scented
June night at the velvet hem of thickest,

pre-dawn black with the barely
perceptible low, round hooting of a

Great Horned Owl declaring
sovereignty in a nearby alder wood.

Lifting me from dream, awake,
the vibration sounded again, closer,

raising hairs on my skin's edge –
instantly conjuring our dark hours

ancient, instinct-sharp terror
of the Presence approaching but unseen.

Wings Against the Morning

Just after sunrise one fine summer morning, I sit
on a favorite chair in a corner of my garden space.

First I hear them – a sibilance of treble tseet-peeps
announcing arrival – and soon small shapes can be seen

flitting through hazel branches and fence-top lattice to
the suet feeder . . . startled at my presence so early,

they sheer off, some diving into shrubs, others veering
sideways, scribing figure eights around the Cape Fuschia –

hunger, though, trumps such skittishness, and first one, then three,
then six settle until eighteen or twenty puff-ball, long-tail

beige bodies are feeding, flittering, pecking each other
on top, sides, inside the wire cage, a dense feathered swarm

of hurry-blurry busyness, always a few turning
about, peering out while voicing those peeping cries. The

sun, lifting higher moment by moment, shines stronger now,
and each feather in this whirligig of fan fluttering-

folding-unfolding wings is back-lit to an alabaster
translucence, calling to mind outspread wings of plump cherubim,

constant attendants on hierarchies of ascendant
angels floating across the springing curves of domed Venetian

ceilings, and I glimpse all these fanned pinions, great and small,
perpetually back-lit as they open against skyscapes of

billowing gold-edged, lilac-gray clouds parting to reveal
that celestial azure lumining Renaissance heavens.

All at once, never ceasing their piping cries, the bushtits
move off in an airy rolling wave of one after

another up-down flight, disappearing into sun-gilded
foliage and leaving not a single downy breast feather

behind – only a sun-burnt retinal after vision of
stainless, out-span wings transparent against morning light.

Garden Vignette with Hummingbirds

A summer day in my small suburban garden . . . I sit
through heat-weighted minutes watching rainbow translucent

petals glowing, green leaves sheening in gilt-bright light while
swallowtail butterfly wanders inconsequent flight . . .

for once no sirens or loud motors on the highway, nor
planes overhead – not even a flutter of birds' wings, or their

usual whistles and calls – only the fountain plashing,
hum of bees browsing scabious, sage, oregano, thyme,

pots of over-spilling annuals, and from a few blocks
away, a blue jay's raucous squawk. Keeping quite still I wait . . .

weaving in-out fence top lattice, a wren begins foraging
earwigs, then mother junco and her young arrive, pecking

at cracks in paving near my feet; piping tseet-peep notes
announce a flurry of bushtits moving into hazel tree then

across to suet cage in feathered, busy-blurry wave;
cross-grained nuthatch honks, drives off chickadees bathing in

hanging water dish so he can drink; as he departs,
female black-headed grosbeak, daringly bold, clamps on . . .

then out from nowhere, a sound of tearing silk –
an iridescent flash slashes through air above flower

beds, atmosphere ions vibrating in its wake – flaunting
his wings' rip-stop sound trick, the male Anna's Hummingbird

is here! Wise to this show-off ruse, I keep from starting, and
after token hover, the vivid atomy lands on

feeder ring, plunging curved beak into a hole, long
tongue setting sugar water trembling slightly. Twice he

pauses to eye the woman in chair less than three feet
away, but she's motionless and he returns to

serious business of refueling. Then above feeder
another male appears, hovers – and Zip! Perched male shoots

after him and both whirl upward, higher, higher, streaking
double helixes in air, then plunge down one-two

so fast my heart near stops in fear of their crash on
pavement. But no – they're up again quicker than blink,

zooming over next yard, streaking farther away. While
they're off, a young female flies straight in, begins sipping

without fuss or glance my direction . . . after drinking
she stands in air inches from my nose, inspecting person

in a pelt the tint of tuberous yellow blooms on
her favorite Cape Fuchsia, closely attending while I

compliment her as a most beautiful, marvelous
creature. Prime male, returned, lands on highest hazel twig

with satisfied mien, preens, settles feathers, starts his one-
note-over-again, clock-work counting.   It might seem presence

of these whizzing whirl-a-gigs – minute dervishes in
feathers effervescing green, cerise, silver and black,

each tiny entity weighing less than a nickel –
couldn't have much impact, yet they affect this little

space beyond all proportion. Spring and summer the male's
unmistakable Geiger counter tick-tick-ticking

counterpoints other birds melodic notes, and signals
another male nearby – or gives notice the way the world

turns not precisely to his liking, and therefore he's of
disposition to chase anything crossing his vision –

I watched a hepped-up male scold flicker on suet
he'd no wish to eat, and chase the larger, flummoxed bird

away — even pursue jay or crow for no apparent
reason, long past nesting season — while demure females

after sipping often hover by me, bright eyes
curious as to my clothes, hair, work amongst the flowers,

while first year juveniles at times suspend in air near
hose arced water, though never yet has one dared to bathe,

however mist-fine the spray. . . . A whiz, arrow-quick, and
this female darts to perch on middle hazel tip while

Alpha male, latest intruder seen off, swears his tick-ticks
from topmost twig then, pleased with himself, begins his

rusty hinge-creak parody of song . . . for thirty
seconds — less — he's content, then another male sheers close,

chittering taunts mid-air — and Alpha is instantly in
hot pursuit . . . the two specks rocket south, then east over

rooftops, disappear. Uncertain, I turn head this way
that, peering near, far. Where? No matter — he'll return —

a sudden surprise unzipping pockets of warm summer air.

White Kite

Engineered intestines of concrete and asphalt strangle
L.A.'s valley, their convoluted curls, twists, torques and loops

continually ingesting-voiding machines fabricated
of metal and plastic that, in their passage, vent poisonous

reeks accumulating to a particulate brown haze
smothering the entire basin, dulling earth's chromatic

spectrum as it creeps west over ocean, east to foothills while
motor and tire noise obscure small sounds of summer life –

rub and scratch of stalk, stem, leaf, bee and beetle whirrs and buzzes,
rabbit and rodent scrapings and nibblings, a coyote's bark.

Forty heart, wing-beats from a freeway, beauty's sudden, stripped perfection:
a white kite hovering over sweep of dry hillside. Shapes pared

to essential: single oak, hill slope, kite above . . . primal colors:
gold grass, cobalt sky, bird's feathers stark white slashed with black – eye
    mask,

primaries, scapula edge – and displayed in tail fanned to stall
forward motion, a flawless balance of blood in bone tension.

A fugitive breeze stirs oak branches, parched dock, poppy stems, bunch
grass stalks, its warm breaths mingling pungencies of dust, seed duff, peeling

bark and manzanita leaves' hot wax with a white-crowned sparrow's
sweet brief song and the faint mewling cries of distant seagulls.

Hawk in Dawn Wind

to G.M.Hopkins wingèd soul

I have seen hawks fly, heads turning, watchful,
against an empty October stained glass sky

curving in domed blue luminescence to
the world's rim, their strong pinions fingering

within the wind, sentient, judging subtle,
elemental harmonies of atmosphere

our earth-bound kind only perceives in tactile
surfaces of things, not spaces between.

Morning bright atoms part, scatter around this
red-tail's flight, swirling glinting mica flakes through

his ascending spirals in the dawn wind rising
between steep white peaks, shadow-sharp crevasses,

slopes of blue-green fir trees and slate gray scree . . .
momently, he hangs suspended in shining air,

outspan wings poised against the gold-fringed, molten
aureole of eastern sun, dark silhouette

swinging stilled until the long second's turn when,
sighting prey, he releases his spine-shivering

primal scream, then hurtles direct earthward,
a god-loosed arrow of swift-feathered death.

Starling Witchery

Autumn wind tumbles piled gray thunderheads,
wild gusts scattering high-spiraling smoke plumes –

screeching, clacking like covens of ancient,
demented hags flying to gruesome midnight

solstice rites, starling flocks swirl upward in a
pitch-iridescent cyclone of ragged witch cloaks . . .

re-descending in whorling funnels of ebon
cinders, the birds, heads jerking, ringed irids

glaring, settle again to frenzied feasting,
needle point yellow beaks piercing, stabbing,

stripping, gobbling clustered blood-red and bruise-blue
berries on rowan trees and elder shrubs.

Hummingbird in Winter

Valiant, small slowed-down heart beating
through ice hard winter hours of

cold and dark . . . after hanging feeder
back out on hook I wait inside

in ghost pale pre-dawn light, relief
immense when I see the prism

feathered atomy fly in, perch
on the thin plastic rim, begin

sipping sugar water. Instants
extend as he drinks without pause, then

lifting head, sits puffed, immobile,
seconds ticking to minutes

before he feeds again. For
a quarter hour his drinking

alternates with periods of rest
for blood-reviving circulation . . .

finally a brief wing stretch and he's off –
this one at least to live another day.

Twelve Sanderlings

A sordid note crawls into the short December
twilight dying in congealed red as we read the three line

news brief: scattered shotgun cartridges on a
Texas beach near bodies of twelve sanderlings.

Only man – kind – could aim to stop a dozen at once of
these shining lives compound of speed and light – their bright
  wings and

silver-quick motions faster than think, more sudden than
seconds but as purposeful in magic transformation

to unexpected other . . . clustered close, the birds rise in
unison – and instantly new creature shaped: a silver-white,

feather-scaled fish of air soars up, plunges down in swift twists
and turns through blue waves of atmosphere before glissading

back onto wet dimpled sand where in an eye blink the shimmer-
scaled form dissolves into a flock of dapple brown-back peeps,

the group lilting forward to surf fringe on thin stick legs,
pausing to stab black beaks for worm or crustacean . . .

after storms, food questing propels scurrying dashes and
darts close to jade ridges of cresting surf, but as the heavy

translucence folds forward, the birds skitter retreat up the
glistening sand till with one mind the flock lifts in a dazzling

whirl of pale wings and white breasts to begin again their fleet
up-rising, down-diving in air above ocean, pinion-scales

of this marvelous feather-fish flickering, glinting in
the pearl-shell radiance reflected between sea and sky.

. . . .

My brain freeze-frames a photo image negative strip:
twelve transparent gray-winged ghosts stalled above a black beach

until, from a mind-impossible height, each begins
a down-turning, slow spiral through ash pale winter sky.

Reality, though, is the sanderlings forward motion stopped
abrupt mid-air, forever less, and the fast, straight drop

of lead-weighted bodies smashing onto a beach where
their blood-smirched broken feathers and small splintered bones

create tiny lightless pyres on the hard-packed sand.

The Wrath of the Anemoi

Birds are killed in thousands in an annual spring
ritual of destruction – thrushes and tiny

warblers in nets and on lime-coated trees, other
species slaughtered by men with guns all across

southern France, down the Italian Peninsula,
Sicily, Libya, Crete, Turkey, Syria,

Egypt, Sudan: hawks and buzzards, stately eagles,
graceful doves, angled cranes, even martins, swifts and

swallows, those daring acrobats of air. The smallest
are blasted to molecular nothing; the larger

birds – the intricacy of hollow bones and layered
perfection of feathers blown apart, thin skin pierced,

weighted by lead shot and no longer sustained
within their native airy element – drop

by hundreds onto stony ridge slopes, weedy
pastures, sand sculpted deserts, empty blue sea.

. . . .

Early in this cruel new millennium, the old wind
gods still at times swooped to favored haunts over

the Middle Sea. . . . They discover the nations of
rainbow-winged beings – the sky-rejoicing flyers sped

on by Boreas, the playfellows delighting to sport with
Notos and Zephyr – sadly diminished, and earth's

enveloping aether so entirely changed even their
substance – vaporous, incorporeal – labors to stay

aloft in a thick murk of inert haze. Where once
supple atoms lightly sustained flight, and vibrant

ions sparked from the millions of small, determined
hearts driving feathered bodies' urgent wings through perilous,

brood-raising days and imperative migrations, now –
lacking the rippling, crossing currents stirred by those

numberless avian wings – there is only oppressive,
monotonous void. Displeased, the Anemoi puff cheeks,

blow up towering, howling tempests that release
tremendous gusts: waterspouts churn the sea, cyclones displace

deserts onto fertile land, hurricanes topple houses,
trees, level cities . . . gathering their attendant breezes,

the sons of Aeolus then rise on enormous, billowing
cloud-indigo pinions, scribing in their lofting ascension

immense black vapor runes across the heavens – and depart
forever earth's barren atmosphere for planets in distant

galaxies enwrapped in more congenial, inhabited skies.

Earth & its Creatures

Votary of Dawn

The poplar stood on the upslope at street's end, ninety
years votary at veiled Aurora's daybreak altar . . .

now only a void – simple air – where once apricot-gold
diffused from sun lifting above the hill spilled

down tree's teardrop lineaments in a radiant
honey pour of light motes lumining every branch

and least twig to the glowing perfection found in
Books of Hours illuminations new-touched by

monks' sable brushes dipped in coruscating, gelid
gold – the hair-fine tips scattering, with precise,

caressing strokes, flames, darts, haloes, rays, sparks of
sun-gilt brilliance over stiff vellum pages.

        . . . .

Each year, April's unfolding yellow-suffused-lime
green leaves triumphed over morning's gold to create

a lacework, transparent scrim in shimmering,
mirror-back chartreuse . . . weeks later, summer-soft winds

stirred currents of ocean coolness through darkening
heart-shape leaves autumn transformed from jade to glowing

amber-topaze shades tossing in equinoctial
gales, the crisped leaf-flakes soon frost alchemized to burning,

brittle embers setting boughs alight, transfiguring
the tree a torch of rustling gold flame, quenched only when

winter's cold sun burnished creaking, naked branches
the rich tarnished gilt of antique picture frames.

        . . . .

The men with saws and machines that kill took a whole
day to reduce you to raw, ugly stump, then days

more to carve and cart your corpse away. Sky there now
barren, its air a bland blank, but I never look

to street's end without seeing your ghost tremble
in that space, bare slim branches swaying in spring

and winter winds, strong limbs rising, in-curved to
each other from your thick forked trunk and forming

a shape of steepled hands, tapered fingers placed
        together, praying. We never listen.

Original Sin

At nine, I stomped honeybees grazing in clover
patches of a grandmother's lawn, accompanied

in causeless cruelty by my brother. At four,
following always where big sister led, he was

guiltless, but for me, though world already out of
joint, no excuses – only a child's viciousness.

Retribution followed a few years later when
we two walked through an alder copse smack into

the hornets' nest boys had whacked from a low branch
onto path – each of the stings received that day so

exquisitely deserved. Now I am overcome
with guilt if I accidently sluice a pin-head size

spider down a drain – how its tiny heart labored
climbing patiently in the dark toward unseen light.

Hell, for me, should be filled with stinging bees –
every jab, prick, stab atonement decades overdue.

Swallowtail

Afternoon splash of wine-gold light across
a mossed rock and plush yellow-brown bee browsing
dark hearts of sunflowers for some reason
brings back myself small, a day I wandered

grandmother's garden: prim white stone edged paths, old,
stout-trunk peach tree, lilies, pansies, daisies,
alyssum – and a giant yellow-striped-black
swallowtail butterfly alighting on my arm.

Astonishment and fear rooted me to the spot –
its body seemed half dragon and its moving
insect feet tickled unbearably – but I
stood statue frozen for long seconds, paralyzed

even this young at beholding close as breath
the tactile, heart-shocking reality of
awesome beauty, yet thrilled to my core it chose
that day to so terrifyingly honor me.

Rat Trap

It was only a small rat, young of its kind,
which somehow made the whole debacle worse.
It hardly had chance to learn wily rat ways,

mate under a summer moon, bring food back to
young in nest. Rats are of course killed every day
by hundreds – traps, poisons, pistols, cats, dogs.

The difference this cool spring night was us –
two people I usually name more than
ordinarily compassionate, and our

decision to kill – decision arising from
belief some kinds of life more worthy than
others – we prefer pleasing-to-our-eyes

colorful, amusing birds to eat the suet, not
ugly, vermin ridden rats, and the cubes of fat,
even in suspended cage, soon caused our small space

to be overrun with rats whose noise woke us,
droppings offended, and worse, damaged treasured
plantings. We began setting 'humane' traps at

night, catching a number with success until
one evening a trap was set somehow awry,
and instead of a sharp snap, it sprang amiss,

catching the creature's thigh, not neck, and for endless
minutes we listened, horrified, while it thrashed
and clung to life with gasping, panting breaths – long

enough for my soul to cringe with guilt and
entire being reject this means of killing.
Who were we to think it our right to decide

which species should survive? Death's trap waits to catch
each of us in its implacable grip – I've
always hoped when those jaws clamp around my life

they will slice with merciful speed, rather
than shaking and squeezing flesh and bone to
slow, agonizing close as happened to that

pathetic rat, expiring miserably in our
garden one May night in a nasty plastic
trap. Next spring though – still much preferring birds

to rats – I suspect we'll set those damn traps
again – and I, by this act, surely forfeit
all honest claim for my own clean, fast end.

Jupiter's Herald

Smoke gray kitten – white mustache, cravat, mittens –
scampers down brick walk in storm portending wind
piling blue-black cumulus over jagged range
of cobalt and alabaster peaks . . . atmosphere

currents shifting, the airy towers begin to
disintegrate, western gusts sending clouds fleeing so
swiftly forward the scudding vapors transform
into streaming plumes that mimic some giant corvid

escaped from ancient myth, while ivory-white snow slopes,
gold-gilt hill and ridge forests, shield-polished silver sound
change from sunlight to shade beneath the great racing
raven-cloud wings. The kitten – ash soft fur ruffling

to thistle puffs, straight up short tail pluming twice size,
eyes all pupil – suddenly pounces where rustle
shivering along dry grass stalks betrays rushing
passage of an outrider zephyr – elusive

herald of the mighty Thunder God's darkling approach.

To an Imprisoned Abyssinian

You crouch on your one perch, gazing with fixed,
yearning unbelief, tail twitching, out the narrow
window framing a sliver of bright

unreachable beyond, the seconds,
hours, days of your life leaking away
with the slow drip of the bathroom faucet.

A prisoner so long (furniture, carpets,
drapes must not be fur-strewn or clawed) when
the woman cages, carries you to

the front room for showing to company,
you run when released, cringe paralyzed and
trembling beneath a chair until caught,

taken back to the safe, small room where
your food, your box, your weeks, months, years
wait, wearing away colorless as

the silent water drops slipping down
the washbowl's bland bare gloss to vanish
from you in a black hole to nowhere.

Evening News – Cat Drowned

The easy solution of eyes filling
with tears at another sorry tale of

man's mistreatment of beasts seems too facile
for you – instead as some sort of crazy

atonement, the shutters of my inward
eye open to replay in recurring
film loops the nightmare of your sorry end.

. . . .

That fearful moment of being thrown, landing
in water asprawl, body weight sinking then

rising, ungainly, heavy with wet – you
turn to swim back, head just above water,

legs, paws frantically paddling, heart thudding
as you labor to attain a shore farther

away each time the man slings you back in –
until that last time, stone tied around your neck,

you sink deeper and deeper, lost from sweet air
and light. A day later the impartial tide

returns you onto grit and crumbled shells, and
soon flies are buzzing above you, crawling on

your stiff matted fur and into your lightless eyes
at the place where you lie – among plastic beer rings,

bottles, metal cans and all the other disregarded
detritus of this incomprehensible world of men.

Lion Eyes

No longer are lions, anywhere, still free,
not even those not penned behind iron bars –

they live in game reserves on limited
acres, and in their roaming sooner than later
arrive a fence marking their territory's end.

Lionesses are held in breeding compounds, coerced
to birth litter after litter of young – cubs, while

growing, are kept in 'petting' parks – attaining full
size, they are released into veldt where hunters garbed in
designer safari gear and clutching rifles shiny

with latest precision mechanisms pay for thrill
of shooting the great beasts from motorized vehicles . . .

a lion's flowing stride carries him fast and far
over grassland, but he cannot outrun a bullet
aimed from an accelerating four-wheel drive.

Living, turning his head to the approaching car,
the lion's gaze is a gate, allowing man to

connect with animal for briefest moment . . .
dying, the complex harmony of striving muscle
and sinew collapses and the lion's eyes become

a dark mirror, giving back reflection of human
predators arriving to stare at, prod, their trophy kill . . .

dead, beating heart stopped, blood pools, black eyes stare, fixed,
unresponsive . . . only a carcass covered in slack,
tawny pelt remains, inert on hard ground – nothing else.

The Last Great Blue

He waits, the last one. It will not be long.

No more the compelled pursuit of chosen mate down
the migration pathways, or calves leaping in spring . . .

no more the lofting buoyancy of tropic waters,
the fountaining falling of sunlit diamond spray

as he heaves his vast bulk up to breech and blow . . .
the sonar voices of his kin echo no more

through the deeps and no others of his species swim
to meet in the long ocean roads. They are all gone,

the sea reaches empty of his kind. An immense
silence pulses through the cold chasms and somber

abysses of ocean, fills the hollows of his
bones and weighs like lead in the chambers of his heart.

He breeches once more, but all primal urgency and
joyous compulsion to lift into air is lost . . .

he begins to sink – down, through translucent gold-flecked
azure, down into darker sapphire shot with

emerald and amethyst gleams, then down still
fathoms lower, beneath the weighted blanket

of thousands of tons of dark water and booming,
pressing silence. His great bulk settles finally on

the sea bed, eyes shut from the intolerable
pressure . . . with enormous effort, he forces

open eyelids, but there is only blackness
stretching to dark forever. His lids close.

His heart beat slows. It will not be long. He waits.

Four Days after the Vernal Equinox, 1989

In Memoriam

Smooth, slippery as a bolt of unfolding watered silk, and with
that same iridescent sheen, the gloss black stream of gelid oil

pours from the tanker breached on Bligh Reef in a fast-flowing unfurl,
becoming in water a thick, clouded shroud enveloping to the

last atom the varied artic life of Prince William's glacier
carved, ice-clear green-blue sound. The salmon would jump, herring scatter,

the grebes, murres, puffins, loons, geese, swans, the harlequin, eider,
ruddy ducks, the otters and seals dive, leave, fly, cry out, but they

are surprised, instantly choked, scales, feathers glued with the ooze, pelts
matted, pores clogged. Hundreds caught in the goop drift to shore where

they pant, inch along or try to flap on the dark-slicked
shingle, wearing out their last hours in silent struggle with imperative

muscle impulse to fly or flee; other thousands – fortunate
perhaps – quickly sink in the fouled water while others wash dead on

oil-slimed rocks. For gorging gulls, eagles, ravens, foxes, bears, death
takes longer, but they too will expire of the stuff, as will the

Sound's entire pod of tuxedo sleek orcas, their joyous leaps
scattering diamond sprays of pure bright water lost forever.

. . . .

Disaster more than thousand miles distant, yet the atmospheric
static bursts generated by the cruelly prolonged dying

of such multitudes of animals, fishes, birds sets off a
constant, flickering interrupt in my mind's circuitry, while

awareness weights heart like stone so many hundreds of pinioned
beings – after navigating perilous, compass drawn day-night

sky routes to breed in blood-decreed nesting grounds – should be doomed
   to
grotesque black death in defiled water and on toxic shingle.

. . . .

This spring I find pleasure dimmed in scents of upwelling sap, cold
blossom, rain softened soil – even delight at returned

acrobat swallows' swooping aerial ballet muted. Through
these days' increasing light, sight and hearing remain oddly

impaired, the accelerating unfurl of leaves, grasses,
plants, the whistles, trills, liquid piping, fluting, warbling of

mate-seeking birds seen and heard as from behind a doubled pane of
window glass. The plain facts – eleven million gallons crude

spilled, thirteen hundred coastline miles polluted – are terrible,
but don't carry photographs' raw shock: oil-drenched otters, seals,

fish and birds piled on sludge-black beaches – hollow-eyed volunteers
washing the few living – a loon, close-up, still alive, wings part

open, feathers pasted to skin, beak agape, red eye wild. I
wish, April Foolish, for a pointed silver stake to pound through

the bloated renascent corpse of the planet's every oil
conglomerate – but only an April Fool could believe

for more than a knife-slice second corporations have hearts –
      they own Public Relations Departments.

Their Steps, Moving Away

Once –
plains, veldts, tundra, forests, woods, jungles, marshes, deltas,
rivers, seas teemed with legions, droves, herds, hosts, multitudes
of mammals and predator beasts. We have slaughtered them

with clubs, harpoons, arrows, sabers and knives, traps, pits, fires
and every kind of gun, human generations killing
and killing – death enough to fill an ocean with blood,

build a continent from carcass teeth and bones. We, and our
children, will see the last pitiful remnants of this
prodigal animal beauty and bounty disappear.

. . . .

I stand on a dry grass verge, watching . . . the great earth mammals
are moving in procession along a narrow path toward
a dense forest. Some step so delicately not one

pebble is displaced: tapirs, reindeer, zebras, horses and
ibex, cheetahs, lions, lynxes, leopards, tigers and wolves . . .
others' steps are ponderously weighted, deliberate –

announcing their approach the ground vibrates: aurochs, bears, bison,
elephants, mammoths, hippopotami, rhinoceros . . .
as the animals reach trees on jungle fringe, the leaves' gossamer

shadow tongues flick over the pelts of thick, luxurious fur –
spotted, striped, velvet swirled – that men killed them for, and the thick
    hides,
wrinkled beige and tan and all gray shades, that early men used,

and the heads, hooves, tails, antlers, horns, tusks tribes of folk ancient
and modern made into fetish tokens, trophy ornaments
or reduced to powder for obscene virility tonics.

As the animals pass farther into the trees, ever denser
umbrageous thickets of sickle and sword shape leaves
and vines obscure them, until, one after another, each is

swallowed entire, vanishing within a wide-gaped gullet
of sound-devouring darkness. Lagging at the chain's bitter end,
a young golden-crested gibbon steps aside, examines

something humped, scaled and dun beside the track, scoops it up with
long arms, stands again. One hand steadying the tree pangolin
on his soft-furred shoulder, the gibbon pauses, half turns his

head, glances back – his eye, liquid, sentient, glints in a
fugitive light mote – then he turns, follows the others into
the hollow, echoless Maw of
                    Absolute
                        Black
                            Extinction.

Plastic Apocalypse

for Barbara

We live on a planet where almost everything has been
touched, smeared, tainted, destroyed by man and his machines –

almost
every inch of prairie, veldt, forest, jungle, ravine, mountain, hill and dale
   trampled, dug, burnt, salted, gouged, ploughed, eroded –
every species of tree axed, chopped, fired, blown up, denuded –
every kind of plant hacked, crushed, torn, smashed, pulped, uprooted –
every marsh, reed bed, delta, shore trash-strewn, dumped with industrial
   effluent and human excrement –
every stream and river polluted, diverted, cemented, dammed –
every lake and sea fished to depletion, poisoned with chemical and sewer
   waste, layered in plastic –

while a rising tide of houses and strip malls inundates
hillsides, woodlands, meadows, valleys, farm acres, bluffs, shorelines.

Most of the large water and land mammals are gone now, or fast
disappearing as territory encroached, or from constant poaching,

fish populations are declining from dams and toxic run-off,
and all bird species – shot, netted, habitat lost – rapidly

diminishing, while the most fragile small creatures are vanishing:
ladybirds, honeybees, dragonflies, butterflies, hedgehogs, tree frogs.

    This is only the beginning of our ending.

. . . .

One soft spring afternoon, my friend walks me to my door –
suddenly she bends, picks up a slight thing showing white on gray

paving . . . silently, as in arcane, ancient ritual,
she hands me the weightless nothing to place in trash. She has

presented me a flake of plastic no bigger than a woman's
thumb – the piece that tears apart when a sack is ripped from

the metal rack of plastic bags at countless check-out counters.

Inner vision watches this lighter-than-feather flake spiral
slowly through space, then sees rising behind, towering leagues high,

a majestic figure in white gathered peplos, sword in one
hand, crowned in wheat-ear coronet: Astraea, virgin daughter

of Titans Eos and Astraeus, holding aloft her paired
golden scales. The plastic flake drifts into the empty dish,

moving it the least degree, as if stirred by exhaled breath or
slightest finger brush . . . the thing settles, sinking bowl to the

precise weight of my friend's blood and bone. But the other bowl is so
grossly overburdened its titanium chains begin distending,

then slip-slide fast downward until arrested scant mile above
jag-edged, coal-black crevasse. Within this enormous, swaying

concave basin, a teeming mass of folk seethe, writhe, gesticulate,
howl, scream, some clambering on piles of broken, bleeding bodies to

peer over rim into the fissure groaning, grinding, gaping
wider every passing second . . . abruptly, the great sword

descends, severs a chain – the bowl tilts, spills the entire
pullulating mass into fathomless depths of fire-lit abyss.

. . . .

'Mene Mene Tekel Upharsin'
burning in phosphor fire, these words once emerged
on an alabaster wall in the palace of a king

. . . .

We too have been weighed in the balance and found
wanting.

Coda
The Stars Beyond

For my part, I know nothing with any certainty, but the sight of stars makes me dream.

Vincent van Gogh

Minerva's Tapestry, Jupiter's Treasure

Regardless whether our eyes will see, even smallest stars set in
black infinity's unfathomed deeps will continue to shiver

fire-spun filaments from their myriad pointed lance tips,
arrowing these scintillae of brilliance – diamond, emerald,

topaze, ruby, aquamarine – through unbounded firmament
that Peerless Minerva, gathering sparks on her twirling distaff, may

spin glistening threads for her eternal weaving of the spangled
girdle of constellations banding earth's night skies. In stately

processional, the goddess's chosen figures, each inwove with starry
gems abstracted from Great Jupiter's immense hoard, unscroll

their tales of abduction, slaughter, revenge, trickery, rescue and
transformation through the seasons, their glittering rays falling

on parallel scenes repeating in lands and kingdoms far below,
again and again, through all the passing centuries of men.

.   .   .   .

Beyond the fraying edges of Minerva's epic zodiac, heaven's
silken sable void expands into limitless god-ruled realms. . . .

There, spectrum-prismed treasure presented by lesser deities
is strewn prodigal over the thousand-stepped plinth supporting
Sovereign Jupiter's monstrous throne.
Coldly, his unappeased gaze surveys the offerings:

immense coffers of gleaming gold spilling seed-pearl star beads in
foaming streams, millions fusing opalescent strings linking paths
through Milky Way as other lustrous swarms cyclone shimmering
forms of galaxy-spanning crowns and brooches –

mammoth titanium chests, silver-shining lids shattering to disclose
revolving stellar bracelets and necklets of moonstone, opal and
zirconium, rotating coronets of solar argentine and vast
swirling rings of glimmering astral dust centered with
   gigantic planetary solitaires —

colossal basalt crater-cauldrons brimmed with crusted volcanic lava,
the seething magma within constantly exploding while flaming
comets blaze forth and whirl into dazzling orbits enwrapping
   chains of fire about the towering pillars of
   All-Seeing Jupiter's luminous throne —

and – prisoned in soaring, serial-splintering, crystal-transparent
vials – atomic motes flashing, sparking, melding into glowing
lightning-twisted platinum torques, each suspending effulgent

pendants of billowing sapphire nebulae, their cumulus
rims irridated with molten radiance, their pulsing, umbrageous
nuclear hearts revealing the endless fissioning, retina-blinding
   white-black-white deaths and rebirths
   of Infinite Empyrean's candescent suns.

Colophon

This book was designed by Jeffrey Copeland at Bywater Press, Bellingham, Washington during the winter of 2016–2017. It is set in Adobe Garamond using the TEX typesetting system.

Garamond is an old-style typeface based on the designs of French typesetter and designer Claude Garamont (1480–1561) early in the age of moveable type. The Adobe version used here was designed by Robert Slimbach in 1989, at the beginning of the age of desktop publishing.

TEX was developed by mathematician and computer scientist Donald Knuth. It was originally released in 1978 and intended for printing mathematical textbooks, however, it is equally suited for high-quality, general-purpose typesetting.

The high-resolution scans of Ms Bayley's art for the section frontispieces were made by Color 1 Photo of Seattle. Djana's cover drawing was scanned at Bywater Press.

www.bywaterpress.com

77215413R00039

Made in the USA
Columbia, SC
18 September 2017